FROM ARMPITS TO ZITS

THE BOOK OF YUCKY BODY BITS

written by Paul Mason illustrated by Mike Gordon

Published in 2013 by Wayland
Copyright © Wayland 2013

Wayland
338 Euston Road
London NW1 3BH

Wayland Australia
Level 17/207 Kent Street
Sydney NSW 2000

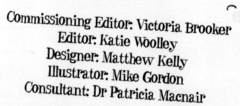

Commissioning Editor: Victoria Brooker
Editor: Katie Woolley
Designer: Matthew Kelly
Illustrator: Mike Gordon
Consultant: Dr Patricia Macnair

British Library Cataloguing in Publication Data

Mason, Paul, 1967-
From armpits to zits : the book of yucky body bits.
1. Human body–Juvenile literature.
I. Title
612-dc22

Illustration copyright © Mike Gordon 2011

ISBN: 9780750279512

2 4 6 8 10 9 7 5 3 1
Printed in China

Wayland is a division of Hachette Children's Books,
an Hachette UK company.
www.hachette.co.uk

CONTENTS

Words in bold can be found in the glossary.

YOU AND YOUR BODY

Your body is a bit like a fortress that's under siege.Outside is the enemy: tiny **organisms** that would really like to get inside, where it's warm and comfortable. Normally, you're good at repelling these attackers but if they get in all kinds of yuckiness can start. The body is also a traitor, making plenty of nasty stuff itself, which is completely normal!

VISIBLE ATTACKERS

There are plenty of tiny creatures that like to make their home on the outer layer of our bodies. Most are microscopic but some you can even see: creatures such as head lice or fleas. These love to make their home on a nice, warm human. Then, whenever they feel hungry, they can have a little snack on your blood!

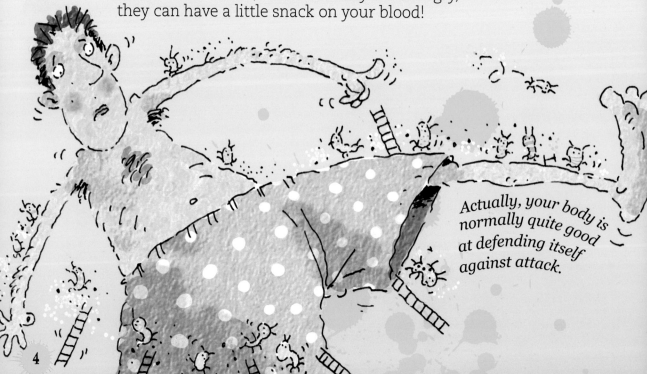

Actually, your body is normally quite good at defending itself against attack.

4

INVISIBLE ATTACKERS

Our bodies are also under attack by tiny creatures we can't see. We only know they are there from their revolting effects! These can include things like:

Our skin starting to smell, or even going scaly and flaking off.

Boils and warts suddenly popping everywhere.

Invisible enemies don't only attack the outside of our bodies. Sometimes they manage to get right inside. If this happens, the yuckiness might include breath that smells like a blocked drain, or **diarrhoea** (uncontrollable, sloppy pooing) which means you dare not venture too far from a toilet.

And if things get really bad, our flesh starts to go rotten!

YUCK!

HEAD LICE AND NITS

Imagine if an uninvited guest moved in, to live among the hairs on your head. Not good – but it gets worse. This guest lives by tapping in through your skin and drinking your blood! It's a head louse: easy to catch but tricky to get rid of.

LICE MANIA!

To a head louse, your head is the perfect hotel and restaurant, all rolled into one. There's plenty of food. All the louse has to do is dig down into your scalp a bit and it can suck up loads of delicious blood. The accommodation is cleaned regularly. True, it's slightly inconvenient when the water sluices through. But lice are excellent at clinging on to a nearby hair, until things quiet down.

HOW TWO LICE BECOME A COLONY...

There's nothing a louse likes more than a big family to keep it company. The louse will lay eggs, called nits, which revel in the warmth of a human head! After about a week, the heat hatches the eggs out into tiny, pinhead-sized lice. Within another week, they are big enough to lay eggs of their own. In a month, just a couple of head lice can get quite a **colony** started!

Look hard and head lice are easily big enough to see.

... AND THEN ANOTHER COLONY

Head lice breed so quickly that they soon run out of space on your head and have to look for somewhere else to live. Fortunately, there are loads of other heads around. Head lice cannot fly, jump or swim. Even so, it takes a louse just 30 seconds to transfer from one human head-hotel to the next. It does this by crawling from hair to hair – very quickly!

GETTING THE GUESTS TO LEAVE

Politely asking the lice to leave won't work – more drastic action is needed! They can be got rid of by:

- **Wet combing with a special comb.**
- **Using a special shampoo or spray.**

Worryingly, though, some lice have now become resistant to the chemicals in the shampoos and sprays!

Head lice are most common in children between the ages of four and 12 years old. It's because they rub their heads together more than anyone else!

DANDRUFF SNOWSTORM

Having dandruff is a bit like being a walking snowstorm. Everywhere you go you leave behind a trail of flaky white stuff. Clothes, the backs of seats, hats and hairbrushes – all end up looking like there's been a mini blizzard nearby.

WHAT IS DANDRUFF?

Dandruff is not, in fact, snow – it is bits of skin that have broken up, then flaked off someone's head. It happens like this:

DANDRUFF MANIA!

Over the years, people have suggested some crazy cures for dandruff:

- Mixing lemon juice, honey and yoghurt, then slathering it over your scalp.
- Whisking together an egg and some baby oil, putting it on your head and letting it dry to a crust, before washing it off.

There's NO evidence that these 'cures' actually work.

The skin on someone's head grows too quickly.

The old skin flakes off and gets tangled in the hair.

The flakes are brushed, shaken, smoothed or otherwise released into the atmosphere.

WHO GETS IT?

The good news is that dandruff is not **infectious** – you can't catch it from someone else. No one is sure why some people get it and others don't. Dandruff is most common among males, teenagers and people in their twenties. It usually affects people during **puberty**, so it may be connected to that. Dandruff has also been linked to oily skin and an overgrowth of a **fungal** yeast that lives on people's scalps (yeuw!).

DUMP THE DANDRUFF

Wishing dandruff away doesn't work – you have to take action! Top tips for dumping the dandruff are:

- **Wash your hair with special anti-dandruff shampoo.**
- **Brush your hair regularly (but not too often! Twice a day is enough).**

If dandruff doesn't disappear, see your doctor, just in case there is something else wrong.

✚

It won't hurt anyone, but a bad case of dandruff is unpleasant and embarassing. Fortunately, it's usually easy to clear up.

GREASE IS THE WORD

Having greasy hair can make you feel like you've got an oil well somewhere on top of your head. The oil well seems like it never stops gushing! Even washing your hair five times a day won't make the problem go away.

TEENAGE TRIPLE WHAMMY

Greasy hair is caused by a greasy scalp. It mainly affects teenagers going through puberty. And, as if greasy hair isn't a big enough problem, it often comes with a side order of greasy skin and spots. What a triple whammy!

WHY DOES HAIR GO GREASY?

Hair grease (its proper name is **sebum**) actually comes from people's skin. We all need a little bit of this grease, which helps protect our skin. But any extra sebum on your scalp quickly spreads along your hair, making it look dull and droopy.

Greasy hair is really annoying – but not as annoying as a little sister who thinks her hair looks great!

RELEASE LESS GREASE!

If only you could just turn off the greasy-hair tap! Unfortunately, it's not that easy – but there are plenty of things you can do:

- Wash your hair each morning with a mild shampoo. But not too often as constantly washing away the grease will make your scalp think it needs to produce more.

- Stop using styling products, such as hair gel. These make it hard for your scalp to work out how much grease it needs to produce.

- Never play with your hair if it's greasy, as this will just cause your scalp to release more grease.

WHO GETS GREASY HAIR?

People with straight hair are most likely to suffer from greasy hair. That's because the grease from their scalp zips easily along the straight hairs. Having curly hair is a good defence against grease – though it might mean you have dry hair instead. (Sometimes, you just can't win!) Annoyingly, brushing your hair is likely to make it greasier, as this spreads grease from the scalp into the hair.

Wash greasy hair regularly to get rid of the grease – just don't get carried away!

ZITS ARE THE PITS

We all know the feeling. You're going out with your friends, you want to look your best and that afternoon – what's this? An uninvited guest on your nose! The biggest zit you've ever seen!

"I'll just give it a quick squeeze!"

WHERE DID IT COME FROM...?

Like all zits, this one happened when grease from your skin blocked a **pore**. Then, bits of dead skin joined the block(age) party, creating a bung. That's when the trouble really started:

Stuff that should have been escaping through your pores (sweat, grease, etc.) got trapped behind the bung of grease and dead skin.

Surrounding skin got red and inflamed.

White blood cells rushed to fight the inflammation (these are what give zits a white core).

As if that's not bad enough, **bacteria** (tiny, single-**cell** life forms) living on the skin may then join the party. Once bacteria get involved, the spot is likely to become **infected** – which means more painful and even bigger. Disaster!

... WHEN WILL IT GO AWAY?

Individual zits will go away on their own. It can be tempting to hurry them along with a squeeze, but this is NOT a good idea! It usually makes the inflammation worse and can cause scarring.

In the longer term, spots are probably caused by the body changes that happen during puberty. Once your body settles into these changes, the zits usually dry up. However, if you're really worried about your zits, go and speak to your doctor about them.

MYTH BUSTER!

Myth 1: Zits are caused by eating greasy food.
There is no evidence that particular foods cause zits. Avoiding greasy food is good for you – but it will not cure zits.

Myth 2: Zits are caused by not washing.
Most of the things that cause zits happen beneath the skin, not on the surface. Washing your face normally, twice a day, is plenty. Use mild cleanser, not soap.

Myth 3: Sunbathing, sunbeds and sunlamps help get rid of zits.
There is no proof that these cut down zits – but there IS proof that too much exposure to sunlight increases the risk of skin cancer.

Myth 4: Zits are infectious.
You cannot catch zits from other people but they are linked to normal bacteria found on the skin.

ZIT RECOGNITION GUIDE

There are four main types of zit:

Blackheads – tiny, blocked skin pores

Whiteheads – little spots with a white 'head' or centre

Pustules – larger redder spots containing lots of **pus**

Nodules – painful under-the-skin lumps with no head (which often appear on your nose just before you go out with your friends)

BOILS AND CARBUNCLES

People often think that boils and carbuncles are the same thing as zits – unless they've had one! If you have had one, you'll know that's like saying a cat and a tiger are the same thing.

BACTERIA ATTACK!

A boil forms when tiny creatures called bacteria crawl beneath the surface of your skin. Our bodies normally defend us from bacteria. Once in a while, though, the bacteria creep below the surface and set up home. Usually they sneak down a hair **follicle**. White blood cells rush to attack the bacteria intruders. Pretty soon, a mess of white cells, dead bacteria and dead skin builds up under your skin. This slowly gathers to form pus, which is surrounded by a hard, red lump and this all causes a boil to form.

WHO GETS BOILS, AND WHERE?

Anyone can get a boil but teenagers and young grown-ups are most likely to have them. Boils usually appear in the places that are moist and oily, which happens to be where they are the most painful and embarrassing:

- face and neck
- armpits
- thighs
- bum

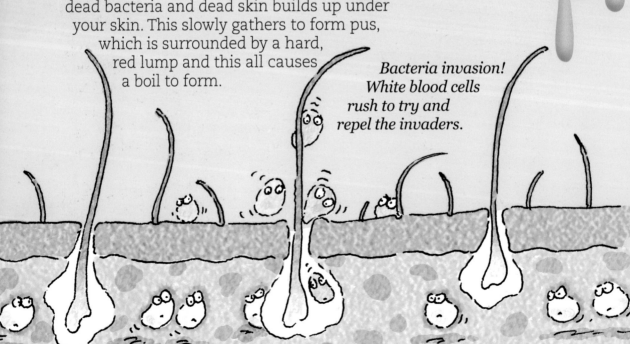

Bacteria invasion! White blood cells rush to try and repel the invaders.

WHAT'S WORSE THAN A BOIL?

If you think boils sound bad, stop reading now – because carbuncles are a lot worse. That's because carbuncles are a gang of boils, linked together beneath the surface of your skin. They have several cores and some or all of them leak pus out of the surface of the skin.

CAN YOU CATCH A CARBUNCLE OR BOIL?

If you know someone with a carbuncle or boil, never touch it. Unlike ordinary zits, they may be infectious. The bacteria that cause them could get on to your skin, burrow down, and start a new infection.

Boils often arrive in a group. Squeezing a boil to make it go away is a bad idea.

BEATING BOILS AND KICKING CARBUNCLES

Most boils heal within a few of weeks, especially once the pus comes out. But some boils and carbuncles require drastic action:

- **Usually the heart of a boil spreads up the hair follicle to the surface, or stretches the skin too tight and it bursts – releasing pus.**

- **Deeply buried boils and carbuncles may have to be cut out and the pus drained away. Ow!**

- **If the carbuncles are larger, persistent or on areas such as the face, you may need antibiotics, so go and see a doctor.**

WARTS AND VERRUCAS

We're all used to the idea that witches (especially evil witches) are warty. But lots of non-witches suffer from warts, too! In fact, studies have shown that as many as one in eight young children and one in four teenagers have warts.

WHAT CAUSES WARTS?

Warts are caused by a **virus**. Viruses are minute organisms, even smaller than bacteria, which live inside the cells of living things. The virus that causes warts is called the human papilloma virus (HPV for short) and it lives in skin cells. HPV causes the top layer of skin to grow too quickly, so that cells pile up and form a rough lump sticking up from the surface.

People with warts or verrucas should cover them up with a plaster before going swimming.

WHEN IS A WART NOT A WART?

When it's a verruca. Verrucas are just warts on the soles of your feet. But because all your weight is pressing down on them, they grow into your skin rather than out from it. Verrucas are the only warts that are sometimes uncomfortable.

ARE WARTS DANGEROUS?

Warts don't look great but they are very rarely dangerous or painful. Even so, get your doctor to check a wart if it bleeds, starts to look different or grows larger.

IS THERE A CURE FOR WARTS?

Warts usually disappear on their own – but it can take years. If you don't want to wait that long, treatments include:

- Treating the wart with a liquid called salicylic **acid**, which usually burns them out within three months.

- The doctor can use a freezing liquid such as nitrogen to kill the cells that make up the wart. They turn into a scab and fall off about a week later.

A doctor knows how to freeze warts and verrucas safely.

CAN I CATCH WARTS FROM SOMEONE ELSE?

Yes, you can easily catch warts by touching skin or even sharing a towel with someone who has them. You can even give yourself warts! Rubbing a wart with your hand, for example, then touching another part of your body can spread the warts around.

MYTH BUSTER!

There are lots of myths about warts – these are just selected highlights:

Myth 1: You can cure warts by rubbing them with potatoes, onions or garlic.

Myth 2: Painting a wart with nail varnish or duct-taping over it will 'kill' it.

Myth 3: You can catch warts from toads.

Myth 4: Warts never stop growing.

NONE of these is true.

17

SNOT AND BOGEYS

Have you ever sat on the school bus in front of someone who's got a snotty cold? The danger is terrible! You never know when they might sneeze and whether a delivery of snot might hit the back of your head as a result!

EXTRA SNOTTY!

When you have a cold, the bits of your nose that produce mucus get red and inflamed. They go into overdrive, to try and protect themselves with a nice, thick coating of snot. Before you know it, there's a waterfall – or at least, a snotterfall – pouring out of your nose.

WHAT IS SNOT?

Snot is the slimy stuff inside your nose. Its proper name is **mucus** and its job is to protect your lungs from things like dust, dirt, germs and pollen. If you breathed these in, they could cause a dangerous infection or reaction, or even clutter up your nice clean lungs. Instead, they get caught up in the hairs and mucus inside your nose. Then they are shoved out either as drippy snot or sticky bogeys or even swallowed (yuck)!

Nasties get trapped in nose hair instead of being breathed into your lungs.

WHAT'S IN A BOGEY?

You'd never eat a bogey if you knew what was in them (even if you're the kind of disgusting person who might have considered it before). Bogeys are made up of mucus, plus the germs, dirt, pollen and other harmful things that get trapped in it before they can cause your body any harm. By eating one, you're just eating all the stuff your body's been trying to get rid of!

Of course, the human body has actually evolved to make use of swallowed bogeys. Our bodies are quite easily able to deal with revolting things like bogies.

Eating a bogey won't actually do you any harm (unless a girl you like sees you doing it!).

DON'T CATCH COLD!

The best way to avoid being snotty is to keep from catching a cold:

- **Keep your nose and throat warm in cold weather.**
- **Don't get too close to people with colds (no kissing!): they are infectious.**

If you get a cold, bring it to a swift end by drinking plenty of water, eating well and getting plenty of rest.

MUCUS MANIA!

- Mucus not only appears in your nose – but also lines your whole digestive system!
- Your body normally produces about a litre of mucus every day!

WAXING UP

Ever looked sideways at a friend or acquaintance – only to leap back in horror at the plug of wax, gleaming yellow from the inside of their ear! What on earth is it and what's it doing there?

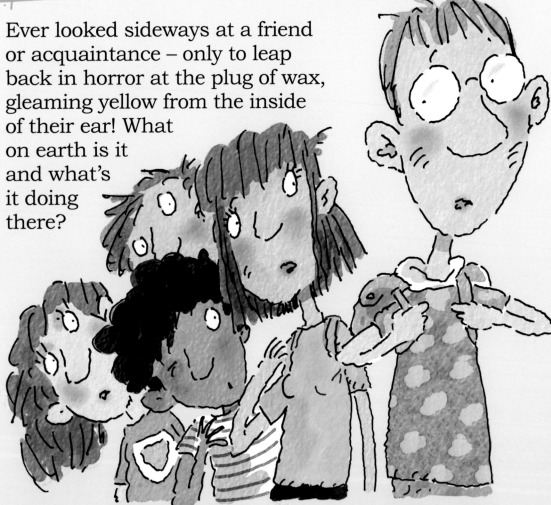

Too much earwax can cause all sorts of problems.

WHAT'S WAX DOING IN MY EAR?

Ears are actually meant to have earwax in them. The wax helps protect your ear canal, the passage that leads from the entrance of your ear to the inner parts. Without earwax, the skin inside your ear would become dry, cracked, infected and sore. So earwax is a good thing!

WHAT IS EARWAX?

Earwax is made up of old skin, waxy material produced by your sweat glands, oily stuff that oozes out of your skin and foreign bits and bobs, such as dirt and pollen.

IS EARWAX EVER A BAD THING?

Too much earwax is sometimes a bad thing. Some of us produce more earwax than others (no one really knows why). Problems start when:

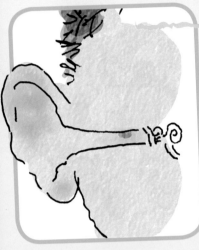

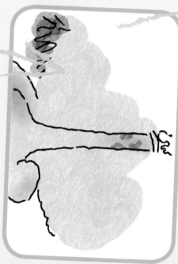

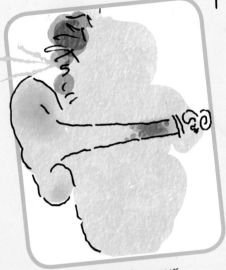

The plug blocks your ear canal.

The wax builds up and goes hard.

The hard wax forms into a 'plug'.

Too much earwax is uncomfortable, may cause a ringing noise in your ears, can reduce your hearing and can even make it feel as if you are constantly about to fall over.

WAX MANIA!

- Earwax has sometimes been recommended for use as lip balm!
- The amount of earwax a whale has increases as it gets older – so you can tell a whale's age by weighing its earwax!
- You can make candles from earwax – but they don't burn very well!

BEATING THE BUILDUP

Putting things into your ear can push earwax into a bung. Every year, millions of people have to have wax bungs removed from their ears. There are several ways of doing this. (NB DON'T try any of these at home!)

- **A doctor could add drops of a special liquid into your ear, which breaks the wax down.**

- **Use 'irrigation', or squirting water down the ear.**

- **Do microsuction, a light bit of ear-hoovering with a tiny hoover.**

- **Perform 'ear toilet', a fancy name for scraping the ear clean.**

BAD-BREATH MONSTERS

Everyone's got one – an uncle or aunt, who insists on giving you a kiss, even though their breath smells so bad it could crinkle crisps. They're suffering from **halitosis** – more commonly known as bad breath.

WHAT THE HECK CAUSES THAT SMELL?

As if the smell of halitosis wasn't bad enough, the cause of it is even worse. The stink is produced by tiny creatures that like to lurk in a person's mouth, especially between their teeth. These creatures are called bacteria – and bad breath is a sort of bacteria fart:

- The bacteria live on tiny, left-behind bits of food.

- As the bacteria break the food down, a stinky gas is released.

- That stinky gas gets breathed out as bad breath.

Sometimes there is no escaping someone with bad breath!

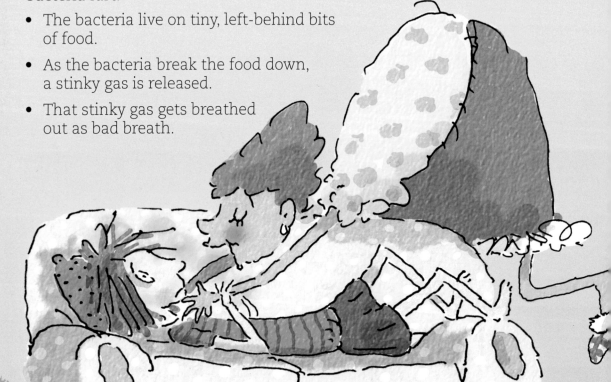

22

ARE THERE OTHER CAUSES OF BAD BREATH?

Smoking, drinking alcohol, eating food such as onions and having a dry mouth can all lead to bad breath. Sometimes it can be caused by illnesses, such as tonsilitis – but if this is the case, sufferers usually have other symptoms, too.

MORNING BREATH

Lots of people wake up with a bit of bad breath. This happens because our mouths make much less **saliva** when we're asleep, so the teeny bits of food left inside them do not get washed away or swallowed down. Instead, bacteria gobble the food up, releasing stinky bad-breath gas.

STOP THE STINK!

The good news is that most cases of bad breath are easy to clear up.

- Brushing your teeth properly, at least twice a day, should brush away the bad-breath bacteria and flossing gets rid of the bits between your teeth.

- Brushing your tongue, which is also home to bacteria, may be a good idea, too.

THE BAD-BREATH TEST

Worried you might have bad breath?

Here's a quick way to check:

1. Give the inside of your wrist a big lick

2. Wait for the saliva to dry and sniff it.

3. If your wrist smells bad, it's time to put a bad-breath cure into action!

FROM PEARLY WHITES TO PEGS

In the days before toothbrushes, very few people over the age of 30 ever gave a big smile. Why? Because everyone would recoil in horror! Where pearly-white teeth used to be, there were only blackened stumps sticking out of their gums.

WHERE DID ALL THE TEETH GO?

All those old pre-toothbrush grins were eaten away by tooth decay. Bacteria – the same kind of tiny creatures that cause bad breath (and boils and carbuncles) – also cause tooth decay. It happens like this:

It just goes to show, you should always look after you teeth!

Bacteria on your teeth form a layer of what's called **plaque**.

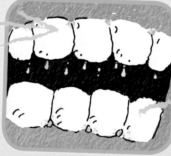

When you eat or drink, the bacteria in plaque also get a meal! While eating tiny bits of food, they create acid.

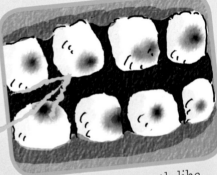

Acid eats away at teeth like warm water being poured on to ice. It also affects the gums. If left unchecked your teeth will rot away and may even have to be removed.

BEATING BACK THE BACTERIA

The reason most of us don't have rotten stumps for teeth, like people in the past, is that we brush our teeth with fluoride toothpaste. This scrubs away most of the bacteria. The few that are left take several hours to rebuild their forces, ready for another plaque attack. In the meantime, the teeth are safe.

MYTH BUSTER!

Through the ages there have been some crazy myths about tooth decay. Here are just three:

Myth 1: Tooth decay is caused by worms.
This idea started because the holes of early tooth decay look a bit like woodworm. It's not true, though!

Myth 2: The more you brush, the stronger your teeth.
Actually, brushing your teeth too much wears away the tooth's hard outer layer and makes rotten teeth more likely!

Myth 3: Having a tooth removed affects your eyesight.
A common myth that is definitely NOT true!

Brushing for three minutes, twice a day, keeps tooth decay at bay.

KEEP DECAY AT BAY

Keeping tooth decay at bay is a constant battle. Here are the key things to do in the fight to keep your teeth:

- Plaque bacteria really LOVE sugar, so avoid lots of sugary food or drink.

- Do not eat between meals – that way, you starve the bacteria into submission.

- Brush your teeth in the morning and before you go to bed for at least three minutes each time, so that bacteria doesn't linger.

ODOUR HORROR

We all know the horror of sitting down next to someone, only to discover that they have a distant relationship with shower gel and deodorant.

Young children rarely suffer from BO but older people who don't wash themselves or their clothes definitely will!

WHAT'S THAT SMELL?

Body odour, or BO, is caused by bacteria that eat sweat. Humans sweat in two ways:

- Through our entire skin.
- Through glands in our armpits and **genitals**.

To BO bacteria, the glandy sweat is like the best-ever steak and a delicious lobster all rolled into one. They can't get enough of it! Unfortunately, as the bacteria chomp their way through the glandy sweat, they produce a stinky acid. Dogs, leopards and other animals with sensitive noses can literally smell it a mile off.

SWEAT MANIA!

- Sweating heavily makes you likely to fail a lie-detector test – people sweat more when lying!
- Human skin starts to sweat at 37 °C: the hotter it gets, the more it sweats!
- Everyone's body odour smells slightly different.

WHERE'S THAT HAIR COME FROM?

Young children do not sweat glandy sweat. It only appears when we enter puberty. At the same time, our voices start changing and our bodies start to look more adult. We also begin to grow hair in odd places, such as our armpits, which can come as a bit of a shock but it's perfectly normal.

WHY DO SOME PEOPLE SMELL STRONGER THAN OTHERS?

Most people who smell simply haven't washed their bodies or clothes enough, which gives the BO bacteria more to munch on. But there are other reasons why people sweat more than usual:

- Being overweight.
- Taking hard exercise.
- Eating hot, spicy food.
- Suffering from some medical conditions, including diabetes or kidney disease.

BEAT THE BO!

For most people, beating BO is relatively easy. These special measures should kick the BO bacteria into touch:

- **Regular washing, with soap and a clean flannel, clears BO bacteria off your skin.**

- **Using an antiperspirant will mean the bacteria have less sweat to eat, so will not produce as much stinky acid and deodorant can control bacteria levels.**

- **Wearing natural fibres, rather than nylon clothes, will mean you sweat less.**

- **Never wearing clothes next to your skin more than once before washing them again, as the sweat smell will be reawakened in them by your body heat.**

In the battle against BO, antiperspirant stops you sweating and deodorant stops you smelling.

27

WIND AND FARTS

What is wind? Where does it come from? And why does it often try to escape from your bottom at the worst possible moment? If you want to know what farts are, how they're made, why they smell and how you can avoid having mighty wind – read on.

WHAT CAUSES FARTING?

Farting happens when gases build up inside your digestive system. There are only two ways they can be released – farting or burping. But where do the gases come from?

They are released by your body as you digest your food or they come from air you have swallowed, down into your gut, instead of breathed in. This happens during eating, especially if you gulp food down instead of chewing it. Chewing gum, sucking on pen tops and smoking also lead to people swallowing a higher-than-usual amount of air.

ARE SOME FOODS MORE FARTY THAN OTHERS?

Some foods contain material that is difficult to digest. This partly-digested food passes through your body, but before being expelled it is broken down by bacteria. One of the side-effects is a lot of extra gas, which has to be farted out. Particularly farty foods include beans, cabbage, artichokes, lentils, prunes, apples and Brussels sprouts.

MEET LA PÉTOMANE

La Pétomane was the world's most famous flatulist or professional farter. He was able to suck air in through his bottom, then fart it back out again whenever he wanted. Amazingly, people would pay money to witness this and between the 1880s and 1914 La Pétomane toured the world's theatres. His act included blowing out candles from several metres away, and playing tunes on an ocarina (a wind instrument) connected to his bum by a rubber pipe.

Oh no!

Sometimes you just can't keep it in!

WHY DO FARTS SMELL BAD?

Actually, most farts don't smell bad – so no one notices them. The stinkers that people do notice happen when your food is not properly digested. The food begins to rot inside you and starts to release sulphur gas. It's the sulphur that stinks.

VOMITING

Vomiting usually happens when your body decides it doesn't like what's in your stomach and throws it out. Often, you don't have much choice about it, apart from having to decide very quickly where to park a delivery of hot, fresh sick.

WHY DO PEOPLE VOMIT?

People's stomachs empty themselves for lots of different reasons. The most common is because they've been poisoned by something they have eaten or drunk. As a defence mechanism, their body decides to get rid of everything in its stomach. This usually happens very quickly!

Sometimes people vomit because they are scared or worried about something. A few people even make themselves vomit deliberately, hoping to lose weight. This is called **bulimia** and is very dangerous.

VOMIT MANIA!

- Whales vomit every week or so, as a normal way of getting rid of things they can't digest! Owls do a similar thing.
- When cats groom themselves they often swallow some fur. This fur is hard to digest, so to get rid of it cats vomit it out!

VOMITING YOUR TEETH AWAY?

Our stomachs contain a lot of acid, which is used to digest food. Whenever you vomit, some of this acid comes up and coats your teeth. If this happens once in a while, the teeth can recover. But people who vomit regularly end up rotting their teeth away. They often end up with false teeth.

WHAT HAPPENS WHEN YOU VOMIT?

When your body decides to vomit, things happen
very quickly and without any help from you:

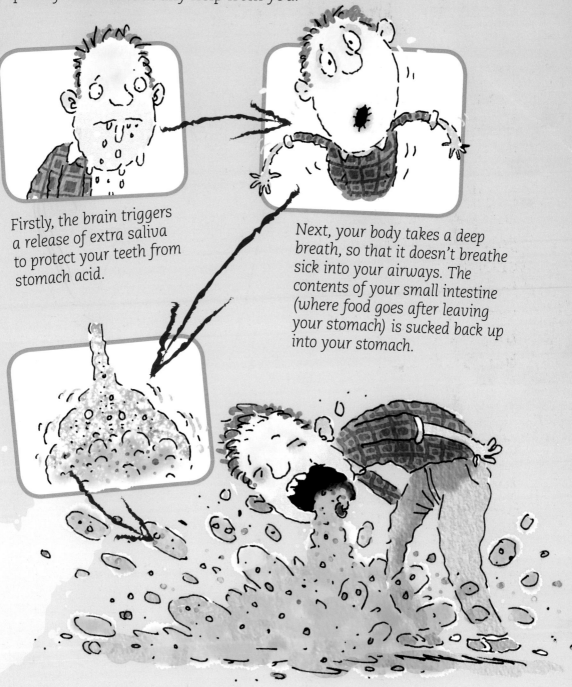

Firstly, the brain triggers
a release of extra saliva
to protect your teeth from
stomach acid.

Next, your body takes a deep
breath, so that it doesn't breathe
sick into your airways. The
contents of your small intestine
(where food goes after leaving
your stomach) is sucked back up
into your stomach.

The muscles in your belly squeeze tightly, forcing the
partly-digested food in your stomach to come shooting
back up into the open air at alarming speed. And if you're
really unlucky, or try to keep it in, some will come out
of your nose as well!

SMELLY FEET

We all know someone who suffers from **bromodosis**. Someone who causes a rush for the exits if he takes off his trainers in the cinema. Someone who's banned from wearing sandals in built-up areas. That's right – bromodosis is the medical name for smelly feet.

SWEATY = SMELLY!

Most people think that their armpits are the sweatiest part of their body – but they're wrong. We actually have more sweat glands in our feet than anywhere else. And just like in your armpits, the sweat attracts hungry bacteria. As they chow down on the yummy (to a bacteria) foot-sweat, smelly acid is produced. The more sweat and bacteria there is on your feet, the smellier they are likely to be.

WHY DO FEET NEED TO SWEAT?

If your feet didn't sweat, you wouldn't be able to play football, dance or do anything else that involved walking or running. Sweating keeps the skin on your feet soft and flexible. If they didn't sweat, the skin would soon become hard and cracked and it may be difficult and painful to walk.

Extremely stinky feet may call for extreme measures.

Warm sweaty feet are ideal places for a bacteria party!

BEAT THE PONG!

Tips for beating the pong if you have noticed that your feet are a bit smelly:

- Avoid shoes that are too tight, hot or made of artificial fibres (so trainers are not good!).
- Wash feet twice a day and dry them carefully.
- Put on fresh socks after washing your feet.
- Always wear 100 per cent cotton socks and shoes made of natural fibres.
- Keep your toenails short, and pumice off any hard skin on the soles of your feet.

WHY DO BACTERIA LIKE HUMAN FEET SO MUCH?

Bacteria just love human feet! First of all, there's plenty of delicious sweat to eat. Second, there are plenty of great places to hang out. Bacteria like it under toenails; the only place they think is better is in the hard skin on the bottom of feet. When the feet get hot, this goes all lovely and soft and the bacteria move straight in!

Don't get down about smelly feet. Washing and drying your feet regularly will help stop them smelling.

ATHLETE'S FOOT

Did you know you could grow mushrooms between your toes? OK, that's not strictly true – but feet can be infected by fungus. Even worse, the fungus can live in your skin. It's called athlete's foot.

WHY'S IT CALLED ATHLETE'S FOOT?

The fungus that causes athlete's foot often lurks on the warm, damp floors of shared showers and changing rooms. The fungus breeds best in hot conditions and athletes often have hot, sweaty feet from wearing training shoes for long periods of time. This means the fungus spreads fastest among athletes: runners, swimmers and people who play team sports in particular. This fungus isn't fussy, though – anyone can get athlete's foot!

It might feel good, but don't scratch or scrape your athlete's foot – it just makes it worse.

HOW DOES THE FUNGUS ACT?

The foot fungus feeds off broken-down, dead skin. It most often affects the skin between your toes but can affect the whole foot. It causes the skin to go scaly, flake and peel off in chunks – sometimes even leaving the flesh underneath exposed. Your foot gets red and itchy. If the fungus really gets hold, you get blisters, your skin starts to crack (very painful!) and it becomes hard to walk. Fortunately, spotting athlete's foot early and treating it stops this from happening.

HOW DOES THE FUNGUS SPREAD?

This fungus hops from person to person quite happily. You have a good chance of getting it if you touch another person's athlete's foot or something like a towel or floor that has been touched by athlete's foot. You might even give it to yourself – the fungus can spread to other parts of the body if you don't wash your hands after touching your feet.

Shared showers and changing rooms are places the athlete's foot fungus loves to lurk.

KICKING ATHLETE'S FOOT TO TOUCH

Fortunately, athlete's foot is relatively easy to get rid of:

- **Wash your feet often with soap and water, then dry them carefully. (DON'T use the towel for anything else or you'll spread the fungus.)**

- **Use an anti-fungus cream or spray you can buy from the pharmacist.**

- **Always wear cotton socks and shoes of natural fibre.**

- **Give your feet fresh air as often as possible.**

MYTH BUSTER!

Myth 1: Peeing in the shower stops you getting athlete's foot.
No, it doesn't, but wearing flip-flops in the shower usually will.

Myth 2: Females can't get athlete's foot.
Males are slightly more likely to get it, but females get it, too.

Myth 3: Putting baking soda in your shoes cures athlete's foot.
It does make the fungus reproduce more slowly, but it won't make it go away.

FUNGUS TOE

The same fungus that causes athlete's foot also causes other foot-related problems. As if scaly, itchy, flaky skin wasn't bad enough! Once the fungus has got itself comfortable in your nice, warm, damp skin, it starts to spread. Pretty soon, it's moved into your toenails and heels, too.

CRACKED UP – BUT NOT FUNNY

If the fungus from your toe spreads to the skin of your heels, the skin becomes dry and hard. Normally when you walk, your weight pushes down on your heel and the skin stretches. Instead, when you have fungus toe, the dry skin splits, like an orange someone has trodden on. At the bottom of the split, you can see the flesh underneath. The splits get so painful, it's hard to walk.

A BAD CASE OF FUNGUS TOE

If you ever spot someone with a toenail that's all white and splotchy, probably with cracks and ridges running down it like a corrugated-plastic roof, they're suffering from fungus toe. Sometimes the nail doesn't turn white. That's not good news, though – instead, it turns black. Or yellow. Or GREEN!

A green toenail is never a good thing!

TACKLING THE TOE FUNGUS

Treating fungus toe can be tricky. Once the fungus has burrowed under your nail, it has an excellent place to hide! One-off attacks, like the sprays and creams that would kill athlete's foot, won't work. Instead, you have to lay siege to the fungus.

Some people try painting anti-fungal paint on to their toenails. The paint seeps through the nail and attacks the fungus underneath.

The best treatment is to take anti-fungal tablets. These get into your bloodstream and hit the fungus through the **nail bed** (the part of your toe the nail is attached to).It takes months before the nail grows completely clear and your toenails are smooth and beautiful once more.

IS FUNGUS TOE INFECTIOUS?

Like athlete's foot, fungus toe is easily passed on to someone else. Never share nail clippers, scissors, foot towels, socks or shoes with a fungus-toe sufferer. Also, using the same clippers or scissors on your un-infected toenails will almost certainly pass the fungus on.

If this girl has fungus toe, she needs to make sure no one else uses those nail clippers. If they do, they'll get it, too.

CURLED AND INGROWN

A really extreme ingrown toenail has to be one of the yuckiest body parts you can ever see. The worst ones are a horror to look at. They are red and swollen as if someone whacked them with a hammer. They may even be leaking foul-smelling pus!

WHAT CAUSES INGROWN TOENAILS?

An ingrown toenail usually happens because the edges of the nail have been cut (or chewed) too short. They grow back into the skin at the side of the toe. But toenails may also do this for other reasons:

- Wearing shoes that are too tight.
- Having very sweaty feet.
- Not washing your feet often enough.

IT'S IN THE GENES!

You're also more likely to get an ingrown toenail if your mum or dad is prone to them. This is thought to be because the shape of your toenails, the way you stand and how you walk are all inherited from your parents.

Wearing tight shoes that squash your toes is one of the causes of ingrown toenails.

IS THERE ANY CURE?

If you spot an ingrown toenail early enough, it can usually be cured at home. Soak the foot in warm water three or four times a day, then gently push the skin away from the sides of the nail. Sadly this isn't a quick fix. You'll need to do this for some weeks or even months.

Ingrown toenails are bad – but they're not THAT bad!

KEEPING TIP-TOP TOES

Avoid the pain of ingrown toenails with these special precautions:

- **Cut your toenails straight across – don't round off the edges. This might be easier after a bath, when the nail will be softer.**
- **Make sure your shoes fit properly*. Too tight or too loose can both cause ingrown toenails.**

*Always buy shoes in the afternoon. Your feet swell up during the day and buying shoes when your feet are biggest makes sure they are not too tight.

DRASTIC ACTION

Really bad cases of ingrown toenail may have to be cured through surgery. Part or all of the toenail is cut out – which can be VERY uncomfortable! The nail bed might even have to be cut out. If this happens, you can wave goodbye to your toenail forever!

MYTH BUSTER!

Some people say that cutting a 'V' shape into the middle of an ingrown toenail will let it grow back together.

NOT true!

TOP TIPS FROM THE TOILET

For centuries, doctors have spent part of their time examining people's poo (faeces). Why? Because the kind of poo you do shows whether your body is processing your food properly, whether you have a good diet and whether you are fit and healthy.

THE POO SCALE!

Experts have developed a special chart for classifying people's poos! They are divided into seven different categories (the poos, not the experts). The categories depend on size, shape and hardness.

CATEGORY 1

Tiny, hard little lumps, like little mini-eggs. These poos are very hard to get out!

CATEGORY 2

Sausage-shaped, but very hard. Category 2 poos are basically joined-together category 1s and are also hard work to get out.

CATEGORY 3

These are sausage-shaped, but smoother than a category 2, with slight cracks visible on their surface. Much easier to get rid of than a category 1 or 2.

CATEGORY 4

This is the smoothest, easiest-to-do poo of all, with a sausage or snake-like shape and a lovely soft consistency.

CATEGORY 5

These are soft, but tend to come out smaller than category 4s.

CATEGORY 6

This poo tends to come out a bit more suddenly than you would like, making it important that you get to the toilet quickly. It will fire out in fluffy pieces, and float in the toilet.

CATEGORY 7

This poo can take you by surprise with its speed of appearance. Easy to get rid of (too easy, in fact), a category 7 will be completely watery, with no solid chunks.

WHAT IT ALL MEANS

Why should you care about what kind of poo you do?

- Category 1 and 2: the poo is staying inside you longer than is ideal. This is called **constipation**. Eat different foods, such as fresh fruit, porridge or bran, to get things moving again. Drinking more water should also help.

- Category 3 to 5: OK, with Category 4 ideal.

- Category 6 and 7: your food is not staying inside your body for long enough, usually because you are unwell. This is called diarrhoea. It is important to drink plenty if you are doing this kind of poo, as your body is losing a lot of fluid!

PEE COLOUR CHART

Just like your poo, your pee (urine) is yucky but useful. The colour of your pee can tell you useful things about how your body is working. An ideal colour is golden yellow. Even more information is available from its smell and – yeuw! – taste.

MYTH BUSTER!

Myth 1: Pee is full of germs
Not true. Pee is completely **sterile** until it leaves the body.

Myth 2: Pee contains harmful substances
Not true – which is why it's normally safe (but not sensible) to drink your own pee, unless you are ill.

PEE MANIA!

- Asparagus turns pee green and makes it smell funny.
- Rhubarb turns it brown!

Doctors used to sniff their patients' pee to try and work out what was wrong with them – and if that didn't work, they'd have a little sip!

PALE YELLOW

Pale yellow pee is perfectly normal. If your pee is this colour, you have nothing to worry about.

BROWN

Brown pee usually just means that you've been eating fava beans, aloe, or rhubarb. If not, though, it can show that you have a liver problem, so a visit to the doctor is needed.

DEEP YELLOW, ORANGE OR AMBER

Mostly this comes from not drinking enough, from drinking coloured drinks or eating carrots, so the urine is very concentrated. Usually, drinking more water quickly gets a nice, healthy pale yellow colour back.

BLUE OR DARK GREEN

Eating a lot of asparagus can turn your pee dark green and some multivitamins or medicines turn it blue. Unless you have taken one of these, green or blue pee means see a doctor.

OILY

Pee sometimes looks oily if you eat lots of fried food. Eating less of these and more brown rice and wholegrain bread will make your pee less oily.

It might be safe, but it wouldn't be very nice to drink your wee!

BODY-PARTS QUIZ

So, from armpits to zits, you know all about yucky body parts. Or do you? Has it all sunk in, like fungus burrowing under a toenail? Or has all that knowledge been blown away like dandruff on a windy day? Take our body-parts quiz to find out!

1. WHY DO LICE LIKE TO HANG OUT ON HUMAN HEADS?

a) Because they love the taste of hair gel.

b) It's warm and cosy and there's plenty to eat.

c) Because they need to have a shower every day and that's a good place to get one.

2. THE BEST CURE FOR DANDRUFF IS:

a) Rubbing uncooked egg all over your head and letting it dry, then peeling it off (while trying not to pull out too much hair at the same time!).

b) Special shampoo made of honey, lemon juice and yoghurt.

c) Anti-dandruff shampoo that you can get from any pharmacy.

3. GREASY HAIR IS MOST COMMON AMONG:

a) Males who are going to go bald before they are 30 years old.

b) Teenagers with straight hair.

c) People who listen to a lot of heavy metal.

4. WHY DO ZITS GET A WHITE BIT IN THE MIDDLE?

a) Because white blood cells are there trying to destroy the zit.

b) So that you can see where to squeeze.

c) Because the flesh in the middle of the zit has died.

5. IS A VERRUCA:

a) An upside-down wart?

b) An ordinary wart, but on the sole of your foot?

c) A sign that you have lots of pet toads?

6. YOU NEED EARWAX IN YOUR EARS BECAUSE:

a) It helps keep your brain warm during cold weather.

b) Without it your ears would fall off.

c) Without it your ears would be cracked and sore inside.

7. WHICH OF THESE BEST DESCRIBE BAD BREATH?

a) A bacteria fart.

b) A sign that someone wears false teeth.

c) The fumes let off by eating too much meat.

8. TOOTH DECAY IS CAUSED BY:

a) Worms that burrow into your teeth.

b) Bacteria that live on your teeth.

c) Eating too much rhubarb.

9. SWEAT-EATING BACTERIA HAVE A FAVOURITE PART OF THE BODY. WHERE IS IT?

a) Armpits.

b) Feet.

c) Both of the above.

10. WHICH OF THESE DINNERS WOULD MAKE YOU FART MOST?

a) Fish and chips.

b) A steak with a bean-and-artichoke salad, followed by prune-and-apple pie for pudding.

c) Spaghetti Bolognese.

11. ATHLETE'S FOOT IS CAUSED BY:

a) Too much running.

b) Wearing lycra too often.

c) Fungus that grows under your skin.

12. THE PERFECT PEE IS:

a) A pale yellow colour.

b) Bright green.

c) Oily and cloudy.

THE ANSWERS

Give yourself a point for each correct answer, then check how your overall score rates:

1 b; 2 c; 3 b; 4 a; 5 b; 6 c; 7 a; 8 b; 9 c; 10 b; 11 c; 12 a.

10 to 15 points – You definitely know your way round the yucky parts of the body, from smelly breath to rotten feet. Congratulations!

5 to 10 points – Not so good, not so good… There's a risk that even the simplest health problem could turn into a bit of a disaster if you're involved. Don't make any health decisions without seeing a doctor first.

0 to 5 points – Oh dear. You must be a dandruff-ridden, spotty, greasy-haired stinker! We suggest you go back and read through this book again.

45

BODY-PARTS GLOSSARY

ACID
sour-tasting liquid that is able to eat away at hard objects

BACTERIA
single-celled life forms, which cause many diseases

BROMODOSIS
smelly feet

BULIMIA
an eating-disorder in which people binge on large amounts of food and then try to empty their bodies of the food by vomiting

CELL
the smallest unit of a living organism; cells are the building blocks from which our bodies are made

COLONY
a group of animals, plants or people that are living together in the same location

CONSTIPATION
when someone finds it difficult to do a poo

DIARRHOEA
a medical problem that causes uncontrollable pooing. The poo comes out as liquid, not solid, material

FOLLICLE
a thin tube in your skin out of which a hair grows

FUNGUS
a tiny organism that absorbs its food from other living things

GENITALS
parts of the body used for reproduction

HALITOSIS
bad breath

INFECTION
an attack on the body by tiny creatures such as bacteria

INFECTIOUS
capable of being passed on from one person to another

MUCUS
clear, slimy material that appears in various parts of our bodies (such as inside our noses)

NAIL BED
living flesh underneath a nail (nails themselves are made up of dead cells, not living ones)

ORGANISM
a living thing such as bacteria or a plant or animal

PLAQUE
a combination of bacteria, saliva, mucus, and food that builds up on the surface of people's teeth if they are not cleaned

PORE
a tiny opening in the skin, which some substances (for example, sweat or grease) can pass through

PUBERTY
a stage of someone's physical development when they start to become capable of having children

PUS
white, yellowish or greenish liquid that appears around an infection. Pus is mainly made of dead white blood cells, bacteria and blood

SALIVA
spit, which is mainly used to make food softer as you chew it. Saliva also contains material that helps protect teeth from acid

SEBUM
an oily material that is released on to the skin to lubricate it and protect it against bacteria

STERILE
free from bacteria

VIRUS
a tiny organism, so small it cannot even be seen with an ordinary microscope, which reproduces inside the cells of other living things. Viruses are responsible for many diseases

UNCOVERING MORE

BOOKS TO READ

Horrible Science: Measly Medicine
Nick Arnold and Tony de Saulles
(Scholastic, 2006)
A gruesome history of medicine,
from trying to cure people by drilling
holes in their heads, to operations
performed without painkillers.

Horrible Science: Deadly Diseases
Nick Arnold and Tony de Saulles
(Scholastic, 2000)
Want to find out about nurses who
drank diarrhoea, doctors who fed
eyeballs to bacteria or how maggots
can clean up an infected wound?
This is the place to do it!

Horrible Science: Deadly Digestion
Nick Arnold and Tony de Saulles
(Scholastic, 2000)
The revolting facts about our digestive
systems: how they work, and
what happens when they don't.
"Absolutely gross" said one young
reviewer – and could there be a
better recommendation than that?

*Open Me Up: Everything You Need
To Know About The Human Body*
Julie Ferris and Philip Letsu
(Dorling Kindersley, 2009)
Just like the title says, this book looks
inside the human body, using artwork
of the bony, squelchy, bloody and
wobbly bits to explain how it all works.

Deadly Diseases and Curious Cures
Anna Clayborne (A&C Black, 2010)
This book focuses on the diseases
and misfortunes that have affected
sailors stuck hundreds of miles out
to sea over the ages. From gangrenous
legs to boils and carbuncles, how did
the ship's doctor sort things out?
Find out here.

WEBSITES

www.childrenfirst.nhs.uk/

This excellent site has been put
together by the world-famous Great
Ormond Street Hospital for Children.
The sections are for children of age 7–11,
12+, and parents and other adults. Each
has an age-appropriate A–Z of health
problems, ranging from spots to
fainting. There is lots of other
information in each section, too.

**www.channel4embarrassingillnesses.
com/teenage-bodies/**

This site has information for
teenagers on some of the body
conditions they might find
embarrassing, how to check
yourself for embarrassing problems
and – of course – plenty of photos
of embarrassing bodies.

**www.nhs.uk/conditions/Pages/
hub.aspx**

Aimed at adults, but this site could
be used by older children who are
confident readers. An A–Z of just
about every medical condition you
can think of – and quite a lot you
can't! There's information on causes,
treatment, and the possible
complications of a
large number of
revolting conditions.

INDEX

Numbers in **bold** refer to illustrations